Step-by-Step Transformations

Turning Milk into Ice Cream

Jerome Hawkins

Cavendish Square

New York

Published in 2015 by Cavendish Square Publishing, LLC
243 5th Avenue, Suite 136, New York, NY 10016

Website: cavendishsq.com

This publication represents the opinions and views of the author based on his or her personal experience, knowledge, and research. The information in this book serves as a general guide only. The author and publisher have used their best efforts in preparing this book and disclaim liability rising directly or indirectly from the use and application of this book.

CPSIA Compliance Information: Batch #WS14CSQ

All websites were available and accurate when this book was sent to press.

Hawkins, Jerome.
Turning milk into ice cream / Jerome Hawkins.
pages cm. — (Step-by-step transformations)
Includes bibliographical references and index.
ISBN 978-1-62713-013-4 (hardcover) ISBN 978-1-62713-014-1 (paperback) ISBN 978-1-62713-015-8 (ebook)
1. Ice cream, ices, etc.—Juvenile literature. 2. Ice cream industry—Juvenile literature. 3. Milk—Juvenile literature. I. Title. II. Series: Step-by-step transformations.

TX795.H38 2014
637'.1—dc23

2014002060

Editorial Director: Dean Miller
Editor: Amy Hayes
Copy Editor: Cynthia Roby
Art Director: Jeffrey Talbot
Designer: Joseph Macri
Photo Researcher: J8 Media
Production Manager: Jennifer Ryder-Talbot
Production Editor: David McNamara

The photographs in this book are used by permission and through the courtesy of: Cover photos by Chris Ted/Digital Vision/Getty Images; Maximilian Stock Ltd./Photographer's Choice/Getty Images; Chris Gramly/E+/Getty Images, 5; Miami Herald/McClatchy-Tribune/Getty Images, 7; © ZUMA Press, Inc./Alamy, 9; Tips Images/SuperStock, 11; Gary Ombler/Dorling Kindersley/Getty Images, 13; Dorling Kindersley Universal Images Group/Newscom, 15; AP Photo/John Heller, 17; AP Photo/Daily Press & Argus, Alan Ward, 19; Inti St Clair/Blend Images/Getty Images, 21; Back Cover: KidStock/Blend Images/Getty Images.

Printed in the United States of America

Contents

Ice cream is made from milk.

The first step is to heat the milk.

The milk gets very hot.

The heat kills **germs** in the milk.

After that, the milk is safe to use.

Next, cream, sugar, and other **ingredients** are added.

Some ingredients are added for **flavor**.

Cocoa is added to make chocolate ice cream.

After that, a **machine** mixes all the ingredients together.

The ingredients form a **mixture**.

Then, the mixture is put in a big vat.

The vat heats and cooks the mixture.

Next, the mixture is put into a cooling tub.

The tub is very cold. It cools the mixture.

15

Now, the mixture is ready to be turned into ice cream.

A machine fills cartons with the mixture.

Finally, the cartons are put into a **freezer**.

Once the mixture freezes, it becomes ice cream.

Ice cream is a delicious treat.

Eating ice cream is a great way to cool off on a hot day.

Words to Know

flavor (FLAY-ver) – the way food tastes

freezer (FREE-zer) – a machine that makes things very cold

germs (JERMZ) – tiny living things that can make you sick

ingredients (in-GREE-dee-entz) – parts that mix together to make a certain thing

machine (muh-SHEEN) – equipment with moving parts that are used to do a job

mixture (MIKS-chur) – something that has several different parts or ingredients

Find Out More

Books

From Milk to Ice Cream
Stacy Taus-Bolstad
Lerner Publishing

Milk to Ice Cream
Julie Murray
ABDO Publishing

Website

Ice Cream in a Bag
U.S. Kids Magazine Website
www.uskidsmags.com/blog/2013/07/19/jack-and-jill-recipes-ice-cream-in-a-bag/

Index